FIND OUT ABOUT

PLASTIC

This edition 2002

Franklin Watts
96 Leonard Street
LONDON EC2A 4XD

Franklin Watts Australia
45-51 Huntley Street
Alexandria
NSW 2015

ISBN: 0 7496 4778 7

Dewey Decimal Classification 668.4

A CIP catalogue record for this book
is available from the British Library

Editor: Annabel Martin
Design: Thumb Design
Cover Design: Chloe Cheesman

Additional photographs:
Royal Botanical Gardens,
Kew/Courtaulds 9, 19;
© Tony Stone Worldwide 18.

Printed in Hong Kong, China

FIND OUT ABOUT PLASTIC

Henry Pluckrose

Photography by Chris Fairclough

W
FRANKLIN WATTS
LONDON • SYDNEY

These garden tools …

these bags and bottles . . .

this cyclist's clothing ...

and these bags which hold tea
have something in common.
They are made with material
which has been manufactured
in a factory.
These man-made materials
did not grow naturally –
like wool on a sheep
or cotton on a plant.

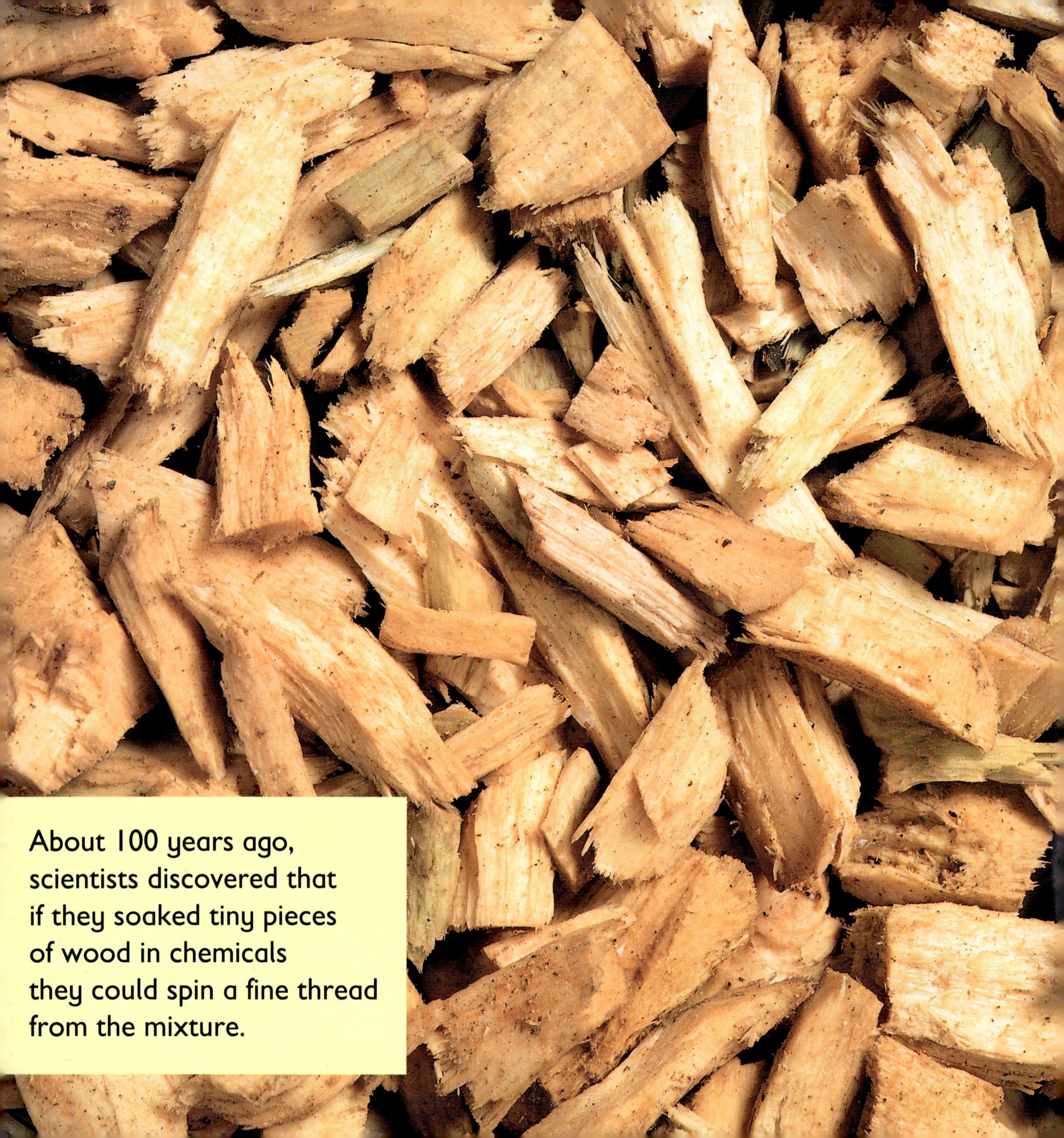

About 100 years ago, scientists discovered that if they soaked tiny pieces of wood in chemicals they could spin a fine thread from the mixture.

They had discovered cellulose.

Cellulose is soft.
It absorbs water.
We use it to make nappies.

Why do you think sponges are made from cellulose?

Cellulose is very tough.
It is used to give extra strength
to tyres . . .

and to make paper wrappings
for food and sweets.
Is cellophane easy to tear?

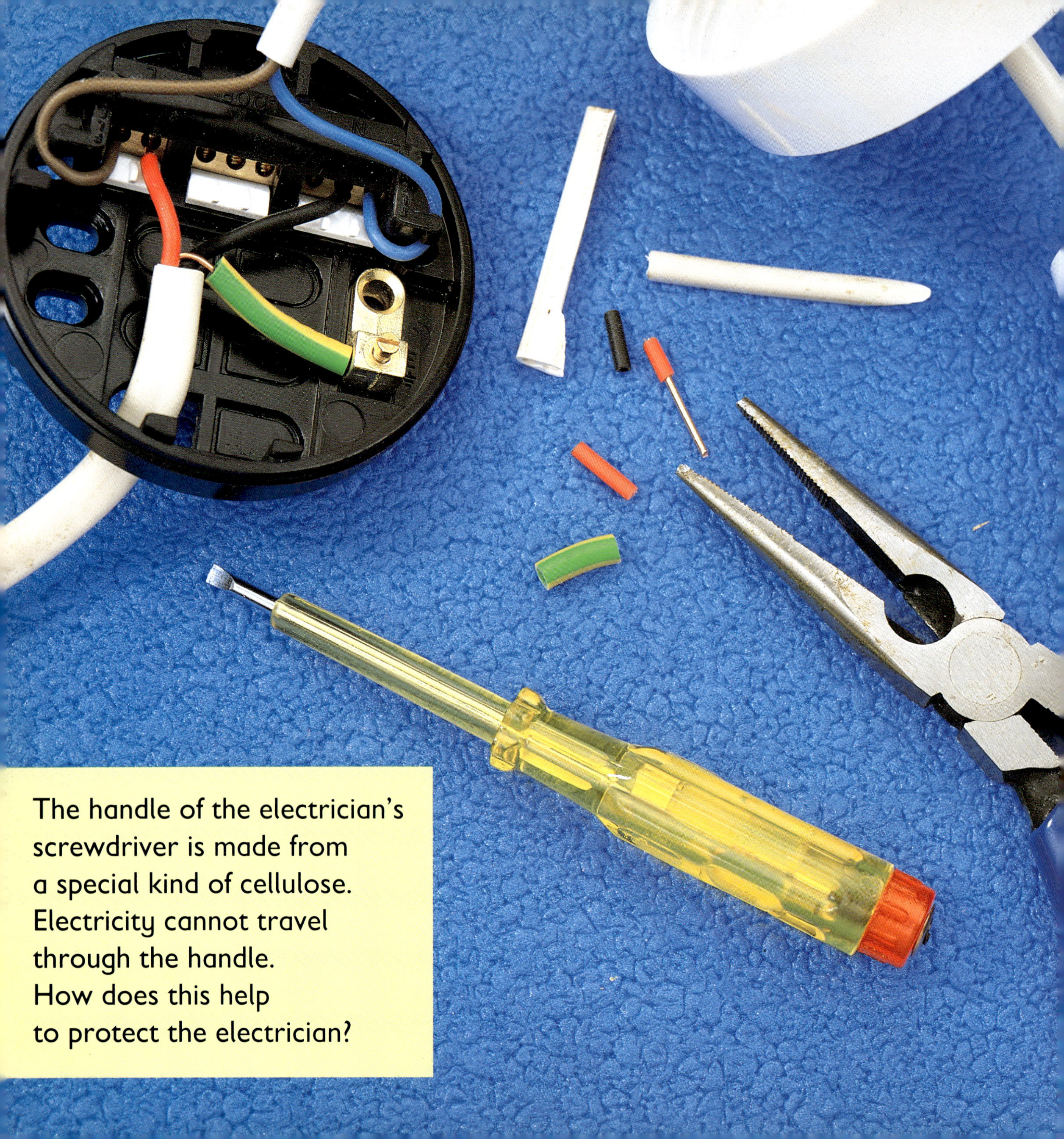

The handle of the electrician's screwdriver is made from a special kind of cellulose. Electricity cannot travel through the handle. How does this help to protect the electrician?

Why does the iron have a plastic handle?

Plastic is a word
which describes an artificial material.
These pots are made from clay
dug from the earth.

These pots are made from plastic. The plastic has been made from chemicals found in oil, gas and coal.

All kinds of things
are made using plastic . . .

even some fabrics.

Plastic is used for the casings of television sets, radios, tape and video recorders. Plastic is light and easy to carry.

Plastic is hard-wearing.
Builders use it for pipes
and guttering.
It does not rot.
It does not need to be painted.

"Polymers" is a word scientists use when talking about plastics made from oil.
Many household paints and varnishes contain polymers.

What is this material called?

Plastics are used in many ways. This pan has a non-stick surface – made from plastic.

Surgeons sometimes need to repair arteries near the heart – with valves made from plastic.

The sky-diver knows
the parachute will support him.
Its cords are made from Nylon –
a type of plastic.

The athlete has to be sure that the pole will not break. It is made of Terylene fibre – a type of plastic.

The hull of this yacht is made of fibreglass – and fibreglass is a type of plastic.

The crew wear waterproof clothes made of PVC – and PVC is a type of plastic.

Many glues, paints, toys, scissors, cutlery, combs pens and rulers are made from plastic.

About this book

This book is designed for use in the home, kindergarten and infant school.

Parents can share the book with young children. Its aim is to bring into focus some of the elements of life and living which are all too often taken for granted. To develop fully, all young children need to have their understanding of the world deepened and the language they use to express their ideas extended. This book, and others in the series, takes the everyday things of the child's world and explores them, harnessing curiosity and wonder in a purposeful way.

For those working with young children each book is designed to be used both as a picture book, which explores ideas and concepts, and as a starting point to talk and exploration. The pictures have been selected because they are of interest in themselves and also because they include elements which will promote enquiry. Talk can lead to displays of items and pictures collected by children and teacher. Pictures and collages can be made by the children themselves.

Everything in our environment is of interest to the growing child. The purpose of these books is to extend and develop that interest.

Henry Pluckrose

But materials like plastic
sometimes bring problems.
They are difficult to destroy.
What do we do
with all the plastic
we no longer need?